P9-CRO-879

WEATHER WATCH

Wind

CAUSES AND EFFECTS

Philip Steele

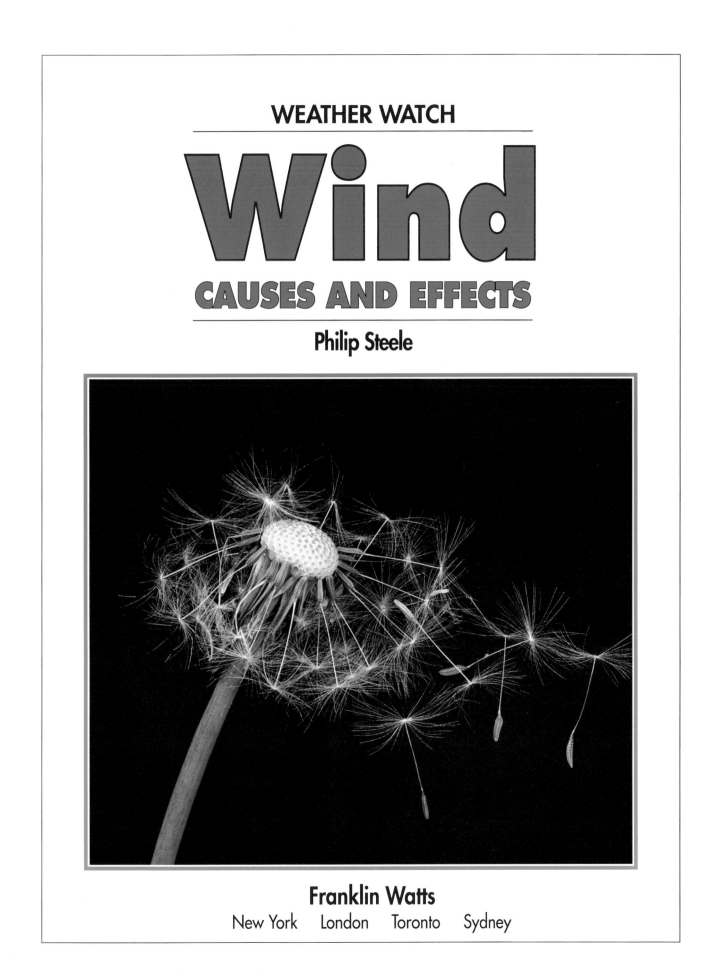

Franklin Watts

New York   London   Toronto   Sydney

Franklin Watts

Library of Congress Cataloging-in-Publication Data

Steele, Philip.
  Wind / Philip Steele
    p. cm.-- (Weather watch)
  Includes index.
  Summary: Describes the various types of winds and their effect on mankind.
  ISBN 0-531-11024-9
  1. Winds-- Juvenile literature. 2. Weather forecasting-- Juvenile literature.
[1. Winds. 2. Weather forecasting.] I. Title. II. Series: Steele, Philip. Weather watch.
QC 931.4.S74   1991   90-46262
551. 5'17--dc20   CIP
                                                                     AC

Printed in the United Kingdom

Design: Jan Sterling
Picture researcher: Jennifer Johnson
Illustrators: Tony Kenyon, Gecko Ltd

Photograph acknowledgements

Cover: (inner) Beken of Cowes Ltd, (outer) S Nielsen / Bruce Coleman Ltd,
p1 L Campbell / NHPA, p3 Robert Harding Picture Library, p4 Robert Harding
Picture Library, p5 Robert Harding Picture Library, p6 Stephen Krasemann /
NHPA, p11 F Damm / ZEFA Picture Library, p13 Mary Evans Picture Library,
p14 Stephen Krasemann / NHPA, p15 Martin B Withers / Frank Lane Picture
Agency, p17 Stephen Krasemann / Science Photo Library, p18 B Harris / ZEFA -
Stockmarket, p19 ZEFA Picture Library, p20 Dave Currey / NHPA, p21 Hans
Dieter Brandl / Frank Lane Picture Agency, p23 Stephen Dalton / NHPA, p25 top
E A Janes / NHPA, p25 bottom F Damm / ZEFA Picture Library, p26 Phillipe Plailly /
Science Photo Library, p26, W K Helmick / Barnaby's Picture Library,
p27 Associated Press, p 28 Tim Davis / Science Photo Library, p29 Sporting
Pictures (UK) Ltd.

Contents

Let the wind blow

The kite was invented in China thousands of years ago and is still popular today with young and old.

Wind gods

The ancient Greeks thought the winds were gods. Boreas was the cold north wind and Notus the south wind. Eurus was the east wind, and Zephyrus the gentle breeze from the west.

A Tower of Winds was built at Athens in the first century B.C. It had a **weather vane** on top, which swung around to show which direction the wind was coming from. It was decorated with sculptures of the wind gods.

There was another Greek god, called Aeolus, who was supposed to control the winds. The Romans made him one of their gods as well. They believed that he lived on the island of Lipari, off the coast of Sicily, where he kept the winds chained up.

No one can see the wind, but everyone can see what it does. If you fly a kite on a windy day, the wind soon carries it high into the sky. You can also feel the wind on your face.

The light winds that we call breezes are welcome on a hot day, helping to keep us cool. They may rustle the leaves, sweep through a field of long grass, and dry the washing on the clothesline. Strong winds can be very powerful and dangerous. People have always feared them because of the damage they can do to crops, homes, and ships at sea.

However, people have made use of the power of the wind for hundreds of years. When sailing ships used to carry cargo across the oceans, a stiff breeze brought the ship into port in good time. People once used the power of the wind to turn the sails of windmills. This power was used to drive machines.

Some traditional windmills, like these in the Netherlands, are still working today.

Some windmills are still used for pumping water. Others are used for grinding wheat into flour. Windmills were first built in the Middle East, in the seventh century. They began to be built in Europe about 500 years later. The wind turned the huge sails, which powered a series of wheels and gears.

What is wind?

◀ Hot gases rise. As long as the gas inside these balloons is kept warmer than the air outside them, the balloons will move upward.

The earth is surrounded by the **atmosphere**, a layer of air about 500 km (300 mi) thick. Although most of this layer of air is made up of a gas called nitrogen, it also contains life-giving oxygen and some carbon dioxide.

There are other gases in the atmosphere as well. When the sun shines on the seas, lakes and rivers, the surface water evaporates and turns into an invisible gas called **water vapor**. As the air near the surface of the earth grows warmer, it rises, taking the water vapor with it. Higher up, the air becomes cooler and the vapor turns into droplets, forming clouds. Lower down, cold air moves in to take the place of the warm air that is rising.

This circulation of warm and cold air is called **convection**, and produces streams or currents of air. All these movements of the air are winds, and the faster the air moves, the stronger the wind blows.

▶ Warm air currents carry water vapor upward as they rise. As the air currents cool, the water vapor condenses. It turns into droplets of water, which are seen as clouds.

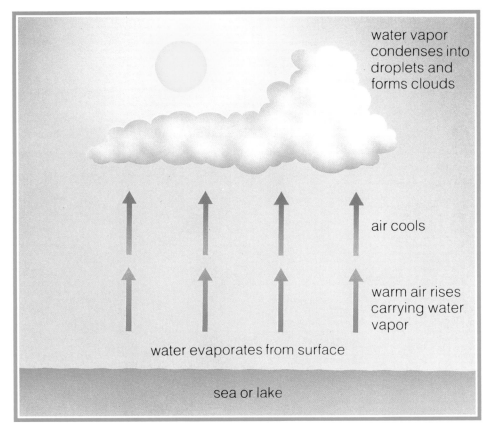

water vapor condenses into droplets and forms clouds

air cools

warm air rises carrying water vapor

water evaporates from surface

sea or lake

The strength of the wind

In 1805, a British admiral called Sir Francis Beaufort worked out a scale of winds for use at sea. The Beaufort scale has since been adapted for use on land and is in general use today.

Force	Type of wind	Effect on landscape	Speed
0	Calm	Smoke rises straight up.	0 kph (less than 1 mph)
1	Light air	Smoke drifts.	1-5 kph (1-3 mph)
2	Light breeze	Leaves rustle; a weather vane moves.	6-11 kph (4-7 mph)
3	Gentle breeze	Twigs move; a flag flaps.	12-19 kph (8-12 mph)
4	Moderate breeze	Dust and paper blow down street; small branches move.	20-29 kph (13-18 mph)
5	Fresh breeze	Small trees start to sway.	30-39 kph (19-24 mph)
6	Strong breeze	Large branches move.	40-49 kph (25-31 mph)
7	Near gale	Whole trees bend over.	50-61 kph (32-38 mph)
8	Gale	Twigs break off.	62-74 kph (39-46 mph)
9	Strong gale	Chimneys crash into street.	75-88 kph (47-54 mph)
10	Storm	Trees uprooted; buildings badly damaged.	89-102 kph (55-63 mph)
11	Violent storm	General destruction.	103-117 kph (64-73 mph)
12	Hurricane	Coasts flooded, devastation.	Over 117 kph (73 mph or more)

Make a wind force scale

You can make your own wind force scale.

Take some strong wire and bend it into an L-shape. The end of the shorter arm should be bent upward as shown.

Punch two holes in a piece of thin cardboard, and use two key rings to attach it to the shorter arm of the wire.

Cut out another piece of thin cardboard and mark it with a curved scale. Draw in, say, 1-6 at equal points on the cardboard. Use a piece of tape to attach the back of the cardboard to the longer arm of the wire.

Put the longer arm of the wire into the ground in a windy position. The wind blows and lifts the flap. How far around does it go? You can read it off against the scale.

Wind and weather

Some winds occur high in the atmosphere. Others move across the earth's surface, where they may be affected by a particular feature of the landscape. Some winds may be funneled between mountains, others forced between tall buildings to swirl around in eddies.

Sea breezes occur along coastlines. During the day, the land warms up more quickly than the sea. The air above the land warms and rises, and colder air from the sea moves in to take its place, causing the sea breezes. At night, the opposite happens. The land cools down more quickly than the sea. The warm air above the sea rises and cold air from the land moves out to sea.

Winds are created along a coastline by the difference in temperature between the land and the sea.

warm air rises from the land

warm air rises from the sea

An Indonesian farmer takes shelter under an umbrella, as the monsoon brings rain to the paddy fields. The summer monsoons are winds that bring rain from the Indian Ocean to the parched countryside of southern Asia.

In southern Asia, the exchange of cold air and warm air between land and sea happens on a seasonal instead of a daily basis. The summer monsoon winds bring cool, moist air from the Indian Ocean. The farmers welcome the arrival of the summer monsoon as it brings torrential rain which they need for their crops.

Highs and lows

The weight of all the gases in the atmosphere pressing down on the surface of the earth is called **air pressure**. Cold, moist air is heavy and creates an area of high pressure. Areas of high air pressure are called **anticyclones**, or just highs. Anticyclones are associated in summer with warm, dry weather because as the cold, moist air slowly sinks, it gets warmer and dries out. In the Northern Hemisphere the wind in an anticyclone circulates in a clockwise direction. In the Southern Hemisphere, the wind moves in a counterclockwise direction. Areas of low pressure are called **depressions**, or just lows. The wind in a depression turns in the opposite direction to the wind in an anticyclone. As depressions move across the oceans and land masses they bring wind and rain.

Around the world

The world's wind patterns are created by the differences in temperature at the equator and the Poles. The wind patterns are affected by the spinning motion of the planet.

The general weather conditions in one area over a long period make up its **climate**. For example, in any one place, at certain times of the year, winds tend to come from the same direction, bringing similar weather. The most common wind in a particular region is called the **prevailing wind**.

Air is on the move around the earth all the time, because warm air rises and cold air stays near the surface. This is what produces the regular pattern of winds on the planet.

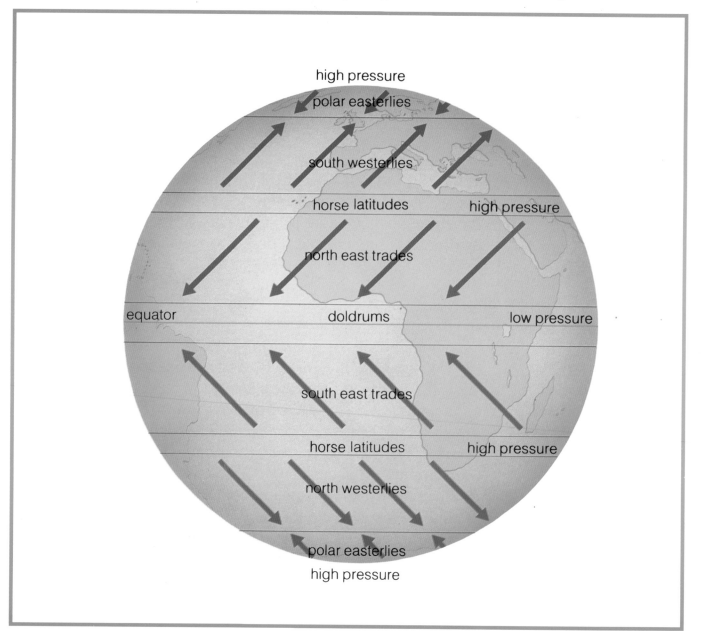

high pressure

polar easterlies

south westerlies

horse latitudes   high pressure

north east trades

equator   doldrums   low pressure

south east trades

horse latitudes   high pressure

north westerlies

polar easterlies

high pressure

Around the equator, the sun shines straight down, warming the earth, which warms the air. The warm air rises rapidly, creating a region of low pressure called the doldrums. The rising air spreads out north and south, finally sinking back to the earth in two regions called the horse latitudes.

Two sets of winds blow from the horse latitudes. The trade winds blow back to the equator. They do not flow directly north-south. Like all other winds they are twisted sideways by a force created by the earth spinning on its axis.

Westerly winds blow polewards from the horse latitudes. In the Southern Hemisphere, the westerlies blow across vast open waters. Between 40 and 60 degrees south **latitude** is a region called the Roaring Forties, where high winds and stormy seas occur. The warm westerlies finally meet cold winds, called polar easterlies, flowing from the poles. Depressions form where warm and cold winds meet.

The fastest of the old sailing ships were known as clippers. They made use of the trade winds to carry cargoes between Europe and Asia. Clippers could sail from London to China and back again in 10 months.

Each year, many people are killed, injured or made homeless by violent hurricanes. Each hurricane is given a code name. The hurricane that caused this damage to a town on the west coast was called Diana.

✳ Hurricanes lose some speed as they reach land, but they can still then be traveling at over 90 kph (50 mph). Their winds often revolve at about 200 kph (124 mph).

✳ In March 1925, a tornado in the central United States killed 689 people and caused great destruction.

Some local winds are famous.

✳ The chinook is a warm, dry wind that descends the eastern slopes of the Rocky Mountains. It sometimes raises air temperatures by 20° C (30°-40°F) in a quarter of an hour.

✳ The mistral is a violent, cold, dry, northerly wind that blows over the South of France for several days at a time.

✳ The sirocco is a hot, dust-laden wind from the Sahara Desert. It blows on the northern Mediterranean coast, mostly in Italy, and on Malta and Sicily.

High winds

Winds of Force 12 and above on the Beaufort scale are called **hurricanes**. Great whirling storms build up around a central area of calm, called the **eye**. Hurricanes can devastate an area as much as 500 km (300 mi) across.

Trees are uprooted, buildings are torn apart, and huge waves are driven against island shores and coastlines. Hurricanes are frequent in the Caribbean and the Gulf of Mexico. In some parts of the world, hurricanes are called typhoons or cyclones. In Queensland, Australia, they are known locally as willy-willies.

The highest winds of all occur in **tornadoes**, whose wind speed can be anywhere from 150 to 450 kph (100 to 300 mph). Tornadoes are narrow whirlwinds of great violence which develop during rotating storms. They can lift a freight car weighing many tons high into the air, or smash a house to pieces. Tornadoes occur most often in the central United States and Australia.

Whirlwinds sometimes carry large amounts of sea or lake water, spinning it around and around to form a **waterspout**. In desert regions sand and dust are picked up by strong winds and carried for hundreds of miles. Such whirlwinds can create sandstorms or form whirling columns called **dust devils**.

Weather lore

Even with modern ships and equipment, the strength and direction of the wind are just as important to sailors nowadays as they were in the days of sailing ships.

Sailors had to be aware of every change in the wind, for gales could drive their ships onto rocks or bring masts crashing down. If there was no wind at all, ships could be becalmed. The sailors believed that if they blew a tune on a whistle, the winds might blow as well.

People on land also had to check from which direction the wind was coming. Towers and church spires were fitted with weather vanes for everyone to see. High winds were not welcomed by farmers. Gales could flatten their crops or blow down barns and haystacks.

This wheat field in Scotland was flattened by high winds. Every farmer fears gales at harvest time.

To remind them about the kinds of weather they could expect, people used sayings passed down from generation to generation. One saying is that:

> March comes in like a lion
> And goes out like a lamb.

This means that the start of the month is marked by roaring winds, but that the end of the month is calm.

> When the wind is in the east
> It does no good to man or beast,

is another saying. Some of these sayings may have been true just for one particular place, and even then were not right all the time.

Make your own weather vane

Find a pencil with an eraser on the end, and stick it point down into a large lump of clay to keep it steady. The vane is made from a plastic drinking straw and some card. Make a slit in each end of the straw. Cut out an arrowhead and tail from the card, and glue them into the slits in the straw.

Then push a pin through the center of the straw and into the eraser at the top of the pencil. Mark north, south, east and west on the clay, then use a compass to position your wind vane on a wall or fence.

Remember: a south wind blows *from* the south, and a north wind *from* the north.

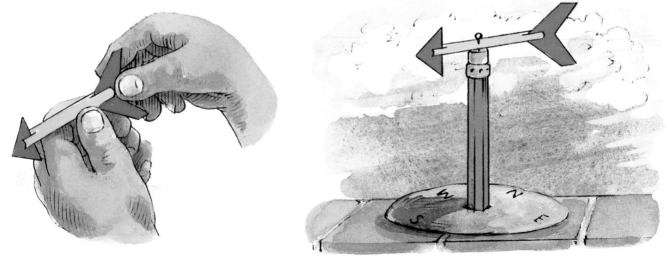

The forecasters

Since the seventeenth century, the scientific study of the weather has been called **meteorology**. However, it was not until the beginning of the nineteenth century that weather conditions began to be recorded every day.

Wind speeds had been measured with simple devices from about 1450, but in 1846 a new kind of **anemometer** was invented which is still in use. It has three or four cups that are attached to a central shaft. The stronger the wind blows, the faster the cups spin around. A dial on the anemometer shows the wind speed.

These meteorologists are setting up instruments which will record temperature, moisture and wind speed. The anemometers whirl around when the wind blows. Every day of the year information is collected about the world's weather. The information is used to make weather forecasts which are passed on to ship and air crews, and to the general public. By comparing the figures over many years, scientists can see if the climate is changing.

Today there are about 10,000 **weather stations** all over the world. The meteorologists use many instruments besides the anemometer to collect and record weather data. **Barometers** are used to measure air pressure and **rain gauges** measure rainfall.

Weather information is also sent to forecasting centers from ships at sea, from aircraft, from balloons released into the atmosphere and from weather satellites. These satellites circle the earth, sending pictures to the weather stations of the winds and cloud patterns moving across the planet.

Mapping the weather

All the information received by the weather stations is fed into central computers, and weather charts are prepared each day. The charts show depressions (lows) and anticyclones (highs), with areas of equal air pressure linked by lines called **isobars**. They also show the borders, or **fronts**, between areas of hot and cold air, as well as temperatures and wind speeds.

The weather reports prepared by the weather centers for ship and air crews have to be very detailed. The forecasts we hear broadcast on radio and television are much simpler. If a particularly violent storm is forecast, such as a hurricane in the Caribbean, special warnings are given, and the movements of the storm are carefully tracked.

✳ The first weather maps were sold in London in 1851, as part of the famous Great Exhibition organized by England's Prince Albert.

Satellite pictures and computers provide this weather forecaster with up-to-date information. He can use it to prepare charts of the weather conditions which may be printed in newspapers or shown on television.

Wind, soil and plants

In stormy weather the wind lashes the earth's surface. The sea is whipped up into huge waves that smash into the coastline, wearing down and **eroding** rock and washing away soil. Wind uproots trees and loosens the soil so that it blows away.

In the same way that the waves are continuously wearing away a coastline, the dust and sand carried by winds in dry regions blast rock surfaces. Rocks are eroded into columns and other strange shapes by the wind.

Wind, heat and water have shaped the rocky landscape of Arizona. The wind has blasted the rock faces with sand and grit, forming arches, towers and steep-sided hills called buttes.

At White Sands National Monument in New Mexico, the wind has eroded a mineral called gypsum from the rocks. This has been blasted into grains of glistening sand and piled into dunes up to 15 m (49 ft) high. In the picture the dunes are covered with patches of snow.

Dust blown from one area may settle in another over the years, forming a crumbly soil called **loess**. This soil is found in China, Central Europe and in the Mississippi Basin. In deserts and on sandy beaches, the wind sculpts the sand into high banks, or dunes. Many of these are constantly on the move, with the wind changing their shape all the time. Wind has a similar effect on fallen snow, piling it into deep drifts and molding it into banks and mounds.

Roots and seeds

The effects of wind can also be seen on plants. In coastal areas trees become twisted and bent over by the prevailing wind. In very open windy areas, on moors and mountainsides, the plant growth is stunted and only low shrubs and heathers can survive. Plants in these places are anchored to the ground with strong, spreading root systems.

Many plants have learned to make use of the wind. The fine, dusty pollen that causes flowering plants to bear fruit is carried by the wind and so are many kinds of seeds. For example, sycamore and maple trees have seeds with flat blades that whirl around as the wind takes them far from their parent tree.

Dandelions have seeds which float through the air on fluffy parachutes. The wind may blow them far away from the plant that produced them.

Wind and wildlife

Most animals shelter from high winds, crouching behind trees or using rocks to protect them. Sometimes their homes may be destroyed by a gale.

Some animals have learned to use the wind for their own purposes. The Portuguese man-of-war, a relative of the jellyfish, has a crested, gas-filled float which extends above the surface of the water and catches the wind, just like a sail. Many animals scent the air while feeding. If one of their enemies is near, its scent will be carried by the wind. The feeding animals are warned and have a chance to escape.

Far and fast

A bird's feathered wings are designed for flight. Air flows over the curved upper wing surface more quickly than under it. Since the air above the wing is lighter than the air below it, the bird flies instead of falling. Flapping the wings helps it to gain height or slow down.

Birds have learned to use all kinds of winds. As hot air currents rise, birds such as the condors of South America soar with them, reaching heights of over 6,000 m (20,000 ft) above sea level. Coastal birds, such as gulls and terns, use the sea breezes, rising and swooping on the switchback currents around high cliffs. Many birds ride the high, fast air currents for speed, then drop down to the surface. When they want to gain height once more, they turn into the wind, like an aircraft taking off.

Migrating birds fly thousands of miles. Arctic terns fly more than 20,000 km (12,000 mi) between the Arctic and Antarctic. They make use of the trade winds and the Roaring Forties for this incredible journey. Albatrosses circle the southern oceans, helped on their way by the fierce gales in that part of the world. Strong winds sometimes blow smaller birds off course. For example, some Asian warblers are even found in the British Isles from time to time, having been blown over 3,000 km (1,800 mi) off course during their migration across eastern Asia.

The kestrel is also known as
the windhover because of
the way it hovers over the
ground, searching for prey.

Riding the wind

The secret of birds' success lies in their feathers, which help them to ride on the wind. Even a tiny bird may have over a thousand feathers, and large birds have tens of thousands.

Start a feather collection. You often see loose feathers lying on the ground. If they are clean and in good condition, pick them up and take them home. You can keep them in an album by slipping them through slits in the pages as shown.

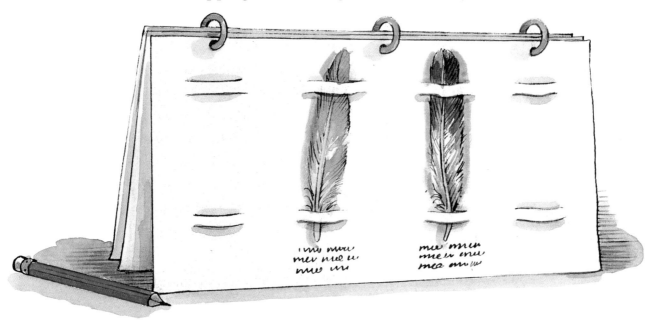

Beside each feather, add a note on where you found it, and whether it is a down feather (the small fluffy ones) or a contour feather (the large ones with horny shafts).

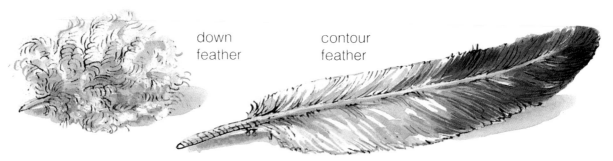

down
feather

contour
feather

Use a book on birds to try to identify which bird the feather may have come from, and add this information to your album as well.

People and the wind

The wind chaps the human skin. It dries it up and cracks it. People who spend all their working lives outside develop skin like leather, tough and tanned.

High winds are often very dangerous. Cars are sometimes crushed by falling trees, and high-sided trucks can be blown over. In the street, people are sometimes hit by falling pieces of buildings or other debris being blown by the wind. At sea, huge waves can swamp small boats, and even large ships are occasionally blown off course onto rocks.

Although light breezes help to keep us feeling fresh and comfortable in summer, in colder weather the wind can carry away our body warmth. This is called **wind chill**.

To be on guard against these dangers, people must always remember the effect of strong winds. For example, people preparing to walk in the mountains or to go sailing must wear warm and waterproof clothing, and make sure that they have food and something warm to drink.

In Northern Europe, sea breezes can be strong. To enjoy a day on the beach, people on Germany's Baltic coast shelter behind wicker work windbreaks.

Building and engineering

Models of high-rise buildings are tested in a wind tunnel. When the machine is turned on, magnesium carbonate powder shows the patterns of turbulence that can be expected around the buildings at different wind speeds. This machine is 4 m (13 ft) wide and 2 m (7 ft) high and produces winds of 100 kph (62 mph).

Bridges, skyscrapers and other high-rise buildings must be able to stand up to hurricane-force winds or higher. When such a structure is planned, a model of the design is made and tested in a **wind tunnel** before building work starts. In the wind tunnel, machines blow air toward the model at high speeds to see how the structure will behave in a strong wind. An additional problem occurs where there are a number of skyscrapers in the same area. The wind is funneled through the narrow gaps between them, and this gives it more force. Bridges and high-rise structures are fitted with anemometers so that people can be warned if the wind is dangerously high. Many bridges have to be closed to traffic in high winds.

The John Hancock Center, Chicago. Its structure includes special "cross-braced" girders on the outside of the building which provide extra strength.

Structures such as skyscrapers are protected against the wind in other ways. They are built of strong materials like steel and reinforced concrete, and they usually have extra steel supports, or cross-bracing, on their sides. Radio and television masts are supported by long cables, or guys.

When the wind blows through gaps and cracks in a building, it creates **drafts**. These mean that heat is lost and therefore energy in the form of fuel is wasted. To avoid such waste, buildings of every kind must be draft-proofed.

Windows can be made draft-proof with double or triple glazing, and doorways can be lined with metal strips. Lining attics with fiberglass also helps to keep heat in a building.

Disasters

The wind caused a terrible disaster in Scotland in 1879. The Tay Bridge collapsed when it was hit by two whirlwinds. A train traveling across it fell into the river and 75 people were drowned.

The wind also destroyed the Tacoma Narrows suspension bridge in Washington State in 1940, although luckily no one was hurt. First the bridge moved slowly up and down, then it twisted, and finally it broke up.

Washington's Tacoma Narrows Bridge was one of the world's great bridges when it was built. However, only four months after its opening in 1940 it was shaken to pieces by high winds. The deck collapsed and fell into the water.

Harnessing the wind

For thousands of years people have used the wind as a source of power. These wind generators are used to generate electricity.

Windmills are rarely used now for grinding grain or pumping water, as they were 100 years ago. However, today, a new type of windmill, called a **wind generator**, is occasionally to be seen on hills in windy places. Wind generators have two or three large blades made of metal. They use no fuel but are powered by the wind. As their blades whirl around, they drive machinery that generates electricity. In California, hundreds of these windmills are built on wind farms and they provide electricity for nearby towns and cities.

Sailing boats still use wind power. Most are small yachts and dinghies, although tall sailing ships are sometimes used for training young people in the old skills. On one modern ocean-going vessel, computer-controlled sails were fitted to the masts so that wind power could be used to help the engines. This experiment showed that fuel costs could be cut in half.

Wind power has always been used for pleasure. Kites and balloons provide entertainment today just as they did in the past. However, it was not until the invention of gliders and aircraft that humans really learned to make use of the winds.

Flying into the wind

For thousands of years, people dreamed of flying.

✳ In 1783, two Frenchmen, Joseph and Étienne Montgolfier, launched the first manned hot-air balloon.

✳ In 1853, an Englishman, George Cayley, built the first manned glider.

✳ In 1891, a German inventor called Otto Lilienthal experimented with a hang glider.

✳ In 1903, two Americans, the Wright brothers, made the first powered flight in a plane.

All kinds of aircraft rely on air currents and wind power. By studying the problems of flight, people have discovered how air moves. This science is called aerodynamics.

Modern aircraft are very different from the wood and wire constructions of the pioneers. Many people have tried to recapture the spirit of adventure of the early days of flight by flying hang gliders and micro-light aircraft, which are small, light structures powered by engines.

The wind can be harnessed for our own purposes, but it can also be destructive. It must never be forgotten that it is among the most powerful forces on earth.

The sport of windsurfing developed during the late 1960s. By 1984 it had become an Olympic sport and was popular around the world. The wind can drive the board over the waves at speeds of over 70 kph (45 mph).

Glossary

air pressure   The force with which the air presses down on the earth's surface at any one point.

anemometer   An instrument for measuring the speed of the wind.

anticyclone, or high   An area of high air pressure bringing dry weather, warm in summer and cold in winter.

atmosphere   The layer of gases that surrounds a planet.

barometer   An instrument for measuring air pressure.

climate   The average weather conditions of a region over a long period.

convection   The movement of heat in a gas or a liquid.

depression, or low   An area of low air pressure, bringing moist weather conditions.

draft   An air current inside a building.

dust devil   A small whirlwind which whips up dust and grit.

erode   To wear away.

eye   The calm center of a hurricane.

front   The border between an area of warm and an area of cold air.

hurricane   A wind blowing at over 117 kph (73 mph).

isobar   A line on a weather map joining points of equal air pressure.

latitude   A horizontal line drawn on a map or globe. Also called a parallel.

loess   A fine, dusty soil carried by the winds from dry regions.

meteorology   The scientific study of weather conditions.

migrate   To travel long distances in order to breed or find a source of food. Many birds and animals migrate each season.

prevailing wind   The wind in any one region which normally blows in one particular direction.

rain gauge   An instrument which funnels rainfall into a container, so that it can be measured.

sea breeze   A local wind, blowing inland from the cool sea to the warm land.

tornado   A narrow funnel of winds whirling around at great speed.

waterspout   A whirlwind over a sea or lake, which carries water in a tall column.

water vapor   An invisible gas which forms in the air when the warmth of the sun dries up water.

weather station   A scientific base where daily weather conditions are recorded.

weather vane   A flat piece of metal, often in the shape of an arrow, which shows the direction from which the wind is blowing.

wind chill   The way the wind rapidly carries warmth away from objects, making them colder.

wind generator   A modern windmill used to make, or generate, electricity.

wind tunnel   A tunnel in which wind forces are re-created in order to test models of aircraft, buildings and other structures that are likely to be affected by the wind.

Index